The Adventures of the Marvelous Monkey Mae :

Monkey Mae taking a rest in some bark mulch after a long hike

Meh ! It's Monday and it's a circus 🐵 around here. Monkey Monday adventures have begun. Daddy's alarm went off at 4:45 this morning he told me he has to go to work so mommy can buy me bows and clothes. Harley hates clothes he won't walk when mommy dresses him up. Bossy only likes the frilly clothes the bigger the better she says. The more flouncy the more bouncy. 🐶 And Me, well you know I'm picture perfect in my bows and clothes oh my !

Anyhow back to daddy leaving for work 😢 . The bad news is I don't have daddy to run to today when the babies get on my nerves.

Do you guys like the races ? 🏎 🏎 🏎 🏎 🐾 🐾 Well... I DO ! In fact I like them so much I showed the babies how to make a race track through the ENTIRE house 🏠

First, I bark at them, then I pounce on them, sometimes I even jump up on the doggy couch, I growl, I snarl, I nip and then when I have irritated them just enough I run 🏃
We go around the kitchen bar, under the dining table 🍽 around the corner and into the living room, up on the doggy couch 🛋, across mommy's feet 👢 bounce off daddy's chair behind the human couch and around and around again and again.

But you know what ?!? This morning when daddy left for work he let the kitty 🐱 inside 🐱. That Cali thinks she is SO SMART. She is always hiding from me, but when I do see her I run up behind her an nip her butt 🐱 , she likes to swipe at me and on occasion she has slapped me across my face she keeps telling me she has sharp nails 🐾 but I haven't seen them.
So this morning during our race 🐾 🐾 🐾 🐾 all 3 of us, myself, Ghost and Coffee bean were enjoying our morning race track race when IT HAPPENED!!! That cat 🐱 jumped out from behind mommy's couch 🛋 and her hair was all funny, standing straight up with her tail all puffy (like me after my bath 🛁) she had the craziest look in her eyes 👀 . 'Bout scared me to death. Then all of a sudden 🐾 🐾 🐾 bam 💥 💥 💥 That Cali got us. Ghost is under daddy's chair, Coffee bean is in the pantry and I am barking at that Cali 🐱 "Who, does she think she is??!!" I keep telling the babies this is a group effort and now I have everyone helping me, mommy said we are too loud, I've got everyone barking 💥 💥 🐾 🐾 💥 💥 and that Cali is hiding. ..... oh wait there she is..Gotta go !

Monkeys Monday adventures have only just begun.....
~ Love 🐾 🐾 Monkey

From left to right -Ghost and Coffee Bean

Hello to all, Monkey here.

I need to tell you all about my morning.

Daddy was up early he had to be out the door before 6 ! I need my beauty sleep 😴. I was not made for this. Mommy got the babies up and out the door we all went. It was rather nice out this morning. I did my normal walk around the house with the others. It goes like this. Bossy (because she's pushy and well... bossy.)Harley because he's the oldest. Then me, The amazing Monkey Mae. Ghost and Coffee bean. We make 3 complete laps around the house. I usually behave until 1/2 way through the first lap, when I get tired of going slow... I want to run ! So this morning I took off like a streak of lightning ⚡ I passed up 🐾 Bossy and Harley, those rascally babies tried to follow me but they tripped and fell over their clumsy baby feets. Mommy waits on the front porch for us. Well as I raced around I was about to turn the corner and pass mommy and GUESS WHAT ?!?! I saw a Peter Cottontail 🐰 I have never seen me a Peter Cottontail in my yard. They usually run out in the pasture with the cows 🐄 and mommy doesn't let me go out with them she says they are too big for me. So anyway back to Mr. Peter 🐰 he saw me and he stood straight up on his back legs. My oh my ! what big ears he had. He shocked me so I stopped running, I skidded to a stop really. My back end swung around and almost bopped myself in the face with my own tail. I sniffed. Mr. Peter sniffed. I wagged my tail. Mr. Peter didn't wag his 😕 I danced forward and stopped. Mr. Peter slammed his feets on the ground. Thump 💥 Thump 💥 So I jumped and my front feets bounced on the ground. Thump 💥 Thump 💥 again ! Mr. Peter wanted to play !!!! I bounced right up to him, I did ! Know what happened next ? Huh, do ya ? Well I'm gonna tell you. Mr. Peter jumped ! Hims jumped so high, he went right over my head. Oh yippee !! Mr. Peter wanted to play leap frog 🐸. Mr. Peter didn't have to show me twice !, GAME ON ! I, the Monkey Mae leap frog grand champion 🏅 was gonna show Mr. Peter !!! He bounced, I bounced. He jumped I jumped . He thumped 💥 I ran right up to his backside and I got him !! He kicked me ! He kicked me ! Miss Monkey Mae queen of mischief and misbehaving! Mr. Peter didn't want to play leap frog 🐸 so I was sad 😢. I hung my head and I went back to mommy, I didn't feel like racing anymore. 🐾 so I think I'll go pout and see how many cookies 🍪 I can get from mommy.

Paws and kisses
🐾💕🐾
~Monkey

Monkey here !

Who likes the circus !? 🙈
I love the circus. 🙈 🐵 🐻 🐨 today I really wanted cookies 🍪 so I thought to myself " Self... how can I get some cookies ?"

Mommy was mopping the living room floor and I spied with my little eyes the bag of cookies 🍪 on the counter. 🐻
I told Bossy... pssssst you want some cookies ? She ignored me.. hmmpt no cookies for her.
I whispered to Harley, hey pops you want some cookies ? He ignored me.
Ghost was all ears literally 🐻 🐵 🐻. I said Ghost... you go sit at mommy's feets and you give your saddest whimper. She might feel bad for you and give us all cookies. He went to mommy and he gave a pitiful whimper and guess what ?, mommy told him he had to wait ! Can you believe that ? Her told the baby to wait !!?!?

So I snuck up on mommy and daddy's love seat and I belly crawled across the back. Whew that was rough, it rocks every inch I inched it rocked trying to knock me off balance. I had to move 🐾 fast, while mommy's back was turned. I inched a long until I could smell the cookies which were just sitting on the counter in their little cookie bag. I stretched like a giraffe 🦒 steady .... steady .... oooooh so close. My mouth was watering 💦 I, the Monkey Mae, tight rope walker expert was sooooo very close to the cookies 🍪 next thing I know, bang, crash, boom 💥 I'm on the floor with the bag of cookies on top of me ! That darn chair wouldn't hold steady and it dropped me on my head. 😣

Good thing our blankie is on the floor by the chair so it didn't hurt when I fell. Mommy laughed at me ! Can you believe that ? Her laughed ! She picked up the cookies and scooped me up too, sure she gave me a kiss and I like those but I really like cookies.

🙈 I still think I'm a good tight rope walker. I'll keep practicing

Paws and kisses
🐾 ·:· 🐾
~ Monkey

> **I WON**
>
> **THIS IS THE LIFE**

Monkey here !

I is very upset ! Do any of you know how to buy an airline ticket ? ✈ 🎫 I need to run away. Do you know what happened to me today ? Huh ?!? Do ya ?!?

Well lemme tell you. I waited all day for daddy to Come home and feed me cookies 🍪 I even wore my tutu for him, and mommy put my piggy 🐷 tails in.

Do you want to know what happened when My daddy got home ? Do you ?

That rascally baby pushed me out of the way and he scratched at MY DADDY'S legs. My daddy picked him up !!!

Daddy did not pick me up first, he picked that rascally baby up ! That Ghost baby climbed right up on daddy's shoulder and perched there. THAT IS MY SPOT ! So I climbed up there and I bit that Ghost right on his rump ! Daddy didn't even get mad, he told

Me I need to be nice to the baby but I have daddy my sweetest look 👀 and he forgave me .

Sure I got some love and a few cookies 🍪 but this is a travesty I tell you ! I need helps, I need to run away and show them that I, the amazing, wonderful, gorgeous Monkey Mae should be picked up first ! No kisses or snuggles for that rascal Ghost ! I should get them all !!

😏 hmmm or how about a sling shot ? Any of you gots one of them ? I could put that rascally Ghost in a sling shot and sling him right outa the room when he tries to sit on daddy's shoulder ! Maybe I should stick to

My first thought, I need a plane ✈ ticket 🎫 . Who will help me ?!?

Paws and Kisses,

Monkey Mae girl who is looking for a travel agent

8

Monkey here !

Today is National Dog Day ! That's what mommy says. It should be National Monkey Mae day, After all I am the queen bee 🐝 🐝 around this house. I've been a semi good girl today, I gots up I played on the hooman bed. Then I heard the shower turn on 🚿 daddy was getting ready for work, I sprung out of bed and ran into the bathroom and right into the shower 💦 🚿 Daddy said "Monkey, what are you doing"? Um 😑 excuse me daddy-o I was making my presence known to you, and here came mommy to take me out of the bathroom. She wrapped me in a towel and dried me off and then I got the monkey zoomies. It was time for the Yorkie 500 down under the bed out the other side, into the living room behind the couch 🛋 up and over the chair sliding around on the wood floor into the kitchen out the other side beneath the dining room table, back to the bedroom and REPEAT !

Mommy said 4:30
Is too early for Monkey Mae Mayhem. I absolutely disagree !
Daddy came out to pack his lunchbox and I watched from my perch on the back of their chair (yeah that crazy one that rocks and dropped me on my head) daddy had this weird contraption that he pulled from the freezer 🧊 he laid it in his lunchbox. He then went into the pantry to get some fruit 🍌 , I made my move ! I leapt and landed right on the kitchen island and peered into his lunchbox. I sniffed, I pawed 🐾 I growled at that blue thing. I nipped it ! BRRRR ! It was cold 🥶 daddy came out of the pantry and he was laughing at me, told
Me I shouldn't be on the island ....but how else am
I gonna see what is going on in his lunchbox ?

Then you know what hims did ? He told me that I could go to
Work with him !! Me ! Monkey Mae could have a work day with daddy !!! I was so excited ! I wiggled, I squirmed, I wagged my tail, I gave daddy lots of kisses to thank him and I was ready to go !! Then !! Then !! Daddy told me he couldn't take me with him without a hard hat ! He didn't want me getting hurt 🥺 . Hims drives big machines, excavators, dozers and other heavy machinery.

Mommy felt bad for me, so I gots a few cookies 🍪 . I held onto her and waved goodbye to daddy. I keep telling mommy to get on Amazon she loves to shop there and get me a hard hat and a safety vest! I, Monkey Mae will be a big heavy machine operator like my daddy.

Well I better run 💨 , time
For a nap 😴 and then cookies and then I'm making an amazon order !

Paws and kisses
🐾 🐶 🐾

~ Monkey Mae

Monkey here !

I've been jailed !!! This is monkey abuse !!! Calling all fur parents and pawed 🐾 friends ! Start a strike ! Protest !! Free Monkey Mae !!

I stole My daddy's socks when mommy was folding clothes. I love his socks 🧦 but only clean ones. I like to steal them and take them to the big dog bed in the living room. I roll on them. I chew on them with my sharp Monkey teeth 🦷 and I drool 😋 all over them 💧. But mommy always catches me ! Today I grabbed them and ran. Up over the back of that crazy chair and it knocked me off balance again !!! It dropped me right into Jail !! Release the Monkey Mae !!

Harley and Bossy didn't care, they circled me laughing 😂 they tried to round me up cowboy 🤠 style so mommy could get the socks 🧦 they aren't too smart 🎓, I was already in jail !!! Mommy tried to give me cookies 🍪 in exchange for the socks 🧦 .... Not even cookies 🍪 could get me out. Socks 🧦 yes, cookies no 🍪

Who will be my pen ✏️ pal 📝 ? Free monkey !!! I'm going to hold out for socks 🧦 !

Soggy socks, paws and kisses

🐾 💧 🧦 💋 ~ Monkey Mae sock bandit

12

Monkey here !!

After my jail experience I thinks my daddy felt sorry for me, he said no more 🧦 socks but I could try a bully stick. Hims bought us all one.

They came today and mommy opened them and gave each of us one.
I've been busy for an hour now, gnawing away I haven't had time to find much trouble.
At first it was a bit chaotic. I went to the big bed, 🛏 bossy went to the chair and Harley to the doggy 🛋 couch. That Bossy she try's to take all the bully sticks. She stole mine, then Harley's and she sats on 'em so we couldn't have 'em.
I barked at her I saids "gimme my bully stick you bully !" She turned her back and kept chewing. Harley hims just gave up and went to take a nap. I, the amazing Monkey Mae was not giving up. I will not be bullied. 😡 😡 😡 I say NO ! To bullies.

Bossy let her guard down and I stole my bully stick back, I ran and jumped onto the hooman 🛋 couch. That Harley missed the whole thing he was really tired 😴.

I never knew something so icky would taste so good ! Mommy said they make her gag 🤢 at the thought of what they are. I do not cares what they are because they are yum yum yummy 😋 in Monkey Mae's tummy ! It's been about 3 hours now and mommy gots all her chores done

☑ and I didn't bug her not once ! Mommy says these bully sticks might be the answer. The answer to what ? I'm confused 😕 anyway yay for bully sticks .

Lots of paws and kisses
🐾 🐾 🐾
~ The marvelous Monkey Mae who stands up to bullies but lays down for bully sticks !

Hellllloo Monkey here !

I decides I needed to fly. I'm so over the crazy chair. Not sure why hoomans like to rock. I gets upset tummy 😖 Since that crazy chair has set out to ruin any attempt I have of getting into something I shouldn't. I decided I need to fly.

Mommy was busy making dinner. Not my dinner but the hooman dinner. I wanted to help. Mommy kept saying Monkey Mae you get down ! And Monkey May you're gonna bonk your head. Monkey Mae ... Monkey Mae. I is da Monkey Mae I knows my name ! I not like Bossy who ignores mommy all the time 🐵 Or Harley who needs hims some old man hearing aids . 👀 oh sorry Harley, yous not old please don't be mad at da Monkey Mae, I'll share my bully sticks wif yous.

Whew ! That was close no one wants Harley mad at dem. He's the oldest a whole 6 !!! Not 6 months like me but 6 whole years that's 42 !!! That's how old my mommy is too. Geez ! Maybes I should get her potty pads if she has em for us wouldn't that mean her needs em too ? 🐵🙈 🐵 Doh ! I got tha look 👀 and a MONKEY MAE !!! So back to flying.... yeah flying

I've got it all figured out! I da Monkey Mae, winged trouble maker. If i's can fly den I can get me bully sticks, and cookies 🍪 and these new things mommy found at pets store 🦴 dems called Himalayan chews they're cheese 🧀 flavored. I thinks 💭 I needs me ones of dems. So here goes up up and away here comes da Monkey Mae !!!

17

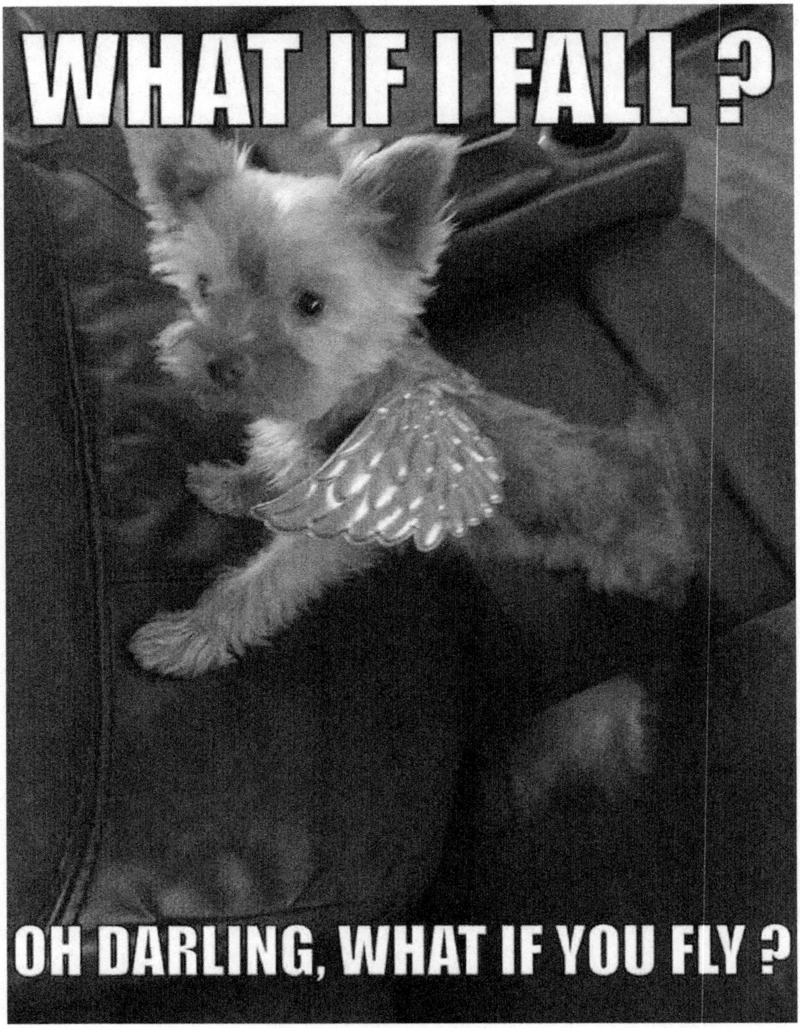
WHAT IF I FALL ?
OH DARLING, WHAT IF YOU FLY ?

Monkey here !

Quick..... paw 1 1
PAW 11 !!

Mommy has lost her marbles.   Like I always knew she was a little bonkers but this ! THIS , takes da cake !!

I was a good girl today, hey don't roll your eyes   I, the fabulous, marvelous, cutie Patootie Monkey Mae was really being good. I even let the dish network guy in the house without raising a stink like Ms. Bossy and Ol'e man Harley did. I needed me some ear muffs with that racket.

Mommy was excited cuz she said our Halloween   costumes came and we all had to try em on. Harley went first. Hims didn't move, he fell over and wouldn't move !!! Mommy said he was being overly dramatic as soon as she took it off he got right up ! Hims crazy
Bossy ran from mommy, her hid under the table and mommy had to move all the kitchen chairs to reach her. She just pranced around thinking her was the best thing since sliced bread .
Does she NOT KNOW ??, who else lives here in this house ?   Tada !! It's me, I lives here too !! Then ! Then ! Mommy picked me up cuz it was my turns to get dressed

I gots me a new tutu I likes it ok, but then came my headpiece !

PAW 11!! PAW 11 !!!
Mommy said I'm the cutest unicorn ever.   I nots a u'horn I a Monkey Mae !!! Somebody help ! PAW 11 !   I need the fur protection services involved!!! I not happy !! I nots going to bark n treat I really not !! not even for bully sticks ! I'm putting my paw   down this time ! Oh wait.... mommy has a bully stick for me, gotta go

Paws and kisses
~   Monkey Mae
Disgruntled Unicorn

Monkey here !!!

Boy oh boy have I had a ruff morning.
It started really early when daddy had to get up at 4:00 am. Mommy let us all outside to go do our businesses. 🐾 💩

We came back inside and I had the crazies. I ran laps and hid under mommy and daddy's 🛏 The kitties 🐱 had come inside to eat some kitty crunchies. Daddy had to call me out and give me my morning time cuddles so I would settle down.
When daddy left, mommy decided she wanted to go back to bed. Hers was tired still 😴
Hers put me into my house, I love my house it's gots super soft blankies and my favorite animals 🧸. Mommy gots into her bed 🛏 hers got all comfy again and then her heard a weird noise.

Mommy sats straight up in her bed. Harley and Bossy were at attention. Then it gots quiet again, so mommy laid back down. Then her heard the kitty 🐱 meow. Mommy got out of bed and went to let him outside, but he was hiding from her. Mommy went back to bed 🛏 again, then her heard lots of noise in my house. Her said "Monkey Mae it's time to go to bed" That Kitty 🐱 hims had other plans, he meowed again. Mommy was really getting frustrated now. She went on a kitty 🐱 hunt but her couldn't find him. He is always hiding from her. Mommy tried one last time to go back to sleep 😴 and crash 💥 my whole house was shaking !!! I thoughts we were having an earth shake !! Mommy jumped out of bed and uncovered my house and opened the door ! That bad kitty was in my house, him was trying to steal my bed 🛏 him made himselfs at home 🏠 in da Monkey Mae mansion !! Hims did a home invasion !!! Can yous believe it ? That had bad kitty 🐱 he ran under mommy's bed and wouldn't come out, we all started barking and mommy was telling us to hush 🤫 her had to go get the broom 🧹 to push bad kitty out then the kitty 🐱 ran out of mommy's room, him ran through the kitchen. Mommy and all of us in hot pursuit 🐕 he ran into the back room, he's fast on 4 legs but mommy was faster 💨 her caught him and put that bad kitty outside.

Mommy gave up trying to go back to bed so we all settled into the chair, and took
A few dog naps not kitty 🐱 naps because I am still upset with the kitty for the home invasion. Mommy said we have to go get ready to go to Grandpas house this afternoon so I gots dressed up in my Monkey dress.
I hope you all have a good Saturday I off to see my grandpa !!
Paws and kisses

🐾 ✨ 🐾 - Monkey Mae a very sleepy girl

Monkey here !

I is so e'cited !!! Sooo excited. Momma has been busy packing our bags, I been supervising her to make sure she doesn't forget nufin.
Monkey dress 👗 ✅
Llama dress 👗 ✅
Unicorn dress 👗 ✅
Snacks ✅
Halter and matching leash ✅
My house 🏠 and my blankies ✅
My favorite animals ✅
😬 shh don't tell her I packed some bully sticks too 🐶 ✅ ✅ ✅ ✅ ✅

We have a long drive 🚗 and thankfully mommy gave me some medicine so hopefully I don't get car sick. 🤢 My hooman brother is going too, hims gets to ride in the backseat wif Harley, Bossy and me !! I, da Monkey Mae carsick queen 🤢 👑 , about to be a beach bum ! But of course while mommy was loading every stuff in da car 🚗 I went for an adventure in the yard. The sprinklers 💦 had just shut off so I went dancing in some muddy spots, I also exercised my lungs by barking at dragon flies and chasing them. Mommy says I have to get my tootsies washed 💧 before we get in da car 🚗. Mommy said it was like trying to catch a flying monkey 🐵 whatever that means. 🙆 I fink mommy should enter me into the Olympics 🏅 🏅 🏅 I betcha I could win the pole vault and da 100 yard dash ! Why ? Cuz I da Monkey Mae, Olympic gold champion of making mommy get a workout without a gym membership.

My daddy is taking us to the beach ⛱ . We gonna walk on the sand and collect some sea shells 🐚 and maybe chase some seagulls. 🐦 🌊

I am sure I will have lots of adventures to tell you all about.

Paws and Kisses,
🐾 ✨ 🐾
~ Monkey Mae
A very tired little girl who needs a nap 😴 so she can dream about 🏖 and hoping she doesn't get carsick 🚗 🤢

Monkey here!!!

Yesterday was not so good in Monkey Mae land. That darn car 🚗 made me very sick 🤢 now mommy says she hasta take it to get cleaned by da professionals. 🧽 I dunno what she's talking about, I, da Monkey Mae and I left her very nice stains all over her tan interior in her new car, even Bossy helped ! We both made sure to miss the blanket she had down for safety at least twice. 😼

Last night we had surf 🦐 n turf 🥩 for dinner. Daddy's friend Mike made bbq oysters they were super yummy and big T-bone steaks with fresh corn 🌽 on da cob. 😋 a huge potato salad that mommy made, her used purple potatoes so the salad looked really pretty, it tasted even better !! We all got to go taste everything. Mommy even let us chew on the corn cobs (with supervision of course) I really liked those they helped my teefs cuz I'm still teething.

There's all kinds of new Monkey friends here. I spent the evening dusk hours barking at deer 🦌 that were eating blackberries right below us. Then I saw a family of raccoons 🦝 🦝 🦝 🦝 who came out from under da deck. Mommy said I could look but not touch dem because they not nice !

Today, daddy and Mike are taking my hooman brother Ryan 🎣. Manya and mommy are taking us to da beach 🏖 and shopping. 🛍 They said if I am a good girl I might get a yummy. I sure hope it's a pup-a-chino or maybe some sea salted bully sticks 😋

I'll get some pictures today. I hope everyone has a beautiful day.

Paws and kisses 🐾 🐾 🐾
~ Monkey Mae

P.S.

Why do they call them seagulls ? Because they fly over the sea if they flew over the bay they'd be called bagels

Paws and Laughter,

Monkey Mae Queen of da Jokes

Monkey here !!!

I is not happy. Not happy at all. Mommy took us to the beach after breakfast 🐵 I had pancakes and they were yummy yummy in my Monkey Mae tummy. We walked the dunes and we were all jumping because the sand was too hot 😫 mommy picked all 3
Of us up and carried us to the jetty. We got to walk on that it was damp from the ocean mist 🌊 my hooman brother and my daddy went fishing 🎣 and mommy walked us !

Guess what we saw ?!?! We saw dolphins 🐬 can you believe it ? They were off shore but they made neat sounds and mommy was really excited, then I saw a crab 🦀 I chased Krusty and hims hid in the rocks of the jetty. I dug at the rocks with all my might but Krusty wouldn't come out of his hiding spot.

I saw seaweed and I know mommy eats it on her sushi 🍣 and I wanted to see what all the fuss was about so I looked at mommy and her was looking out at the 🌊 ocean. I slowly slowly stuck my tongue 👅 out to taste it and just as I get a taste, mommy says "Monkey Mae NO !" Geez I know my name, and seaweed is yucky ! I don't know what mommy is thinking eating that stuff.
😤

Then we went for ice cream 🍦 and you know what the ice cream man told mommy ?!? Hims said they have doggie ice cream 🍨 I begged her, I stood on my back legs and did my best Monkey Mae dance and all the peoples were clapping 👏 thems was clapping for me ! Me, I da dancing for ice cream 🍦 Monkey Mae ! The man asked mommy if we could all have some and she said YES !! Monkey Mae gots an ice cream, well he called it a pupsicle it was so nummy.
😌

But then ! Then Mommy said we had to go because we had a 5 hour drive. I is not happy, not happy at all. We went back to the jetty to pick up daddy and brother and I was fussin so mommy wrapped me in a blanket and patted me her was telling us how proud she was of all of us for being so good. I hope we can go again really soon. I decided I love the beach 🏖 but now I am one tired 😩 little Monkey Mae.

Paws and kisses
🐾 🐾 🐾
~Monkey Mae
Ice cream queen 🍦 👑

Monkey here !!

I knows I've told you that my mommy is bonkers 😜 🐒 and if you didn't believe me before you might now. 😂 This might be TMMI (Too Much Monkey Information) but when we traveled to the beach ⛱ Bossy and I refused to go potty. 💩 Even if mommy offered treats it wasn't happening. 🍪

Mommy was worried 😟 that Bossy and I were gonna get bound up. She knows we don't like mineral oil 😝 but she said she would give it to us if she had to.

Her is crazy 😜 she followed us all around today with her eagle eyes. 👁 👀
We just wanted to go potty in peace. It's totally ok if WE follow her to the bathroom 🚽 🧻 🚽 🚿

And lay in wait with our beady little eyes 👀 👀 👀 staring at her. Why 🙄 can't we potty alone ?
🌱 💩 🌱

Anyhoo, back to me and Bossy. Mommy was following us all day long. Her was checking if she needed to get the mineral oil 😝 Bossy and I finally went potty 💩 and mommy freaked out !!!
🏠🏃‍♀️🐕‍🦺🐕🏠🏥🏃‍♀️🐕🏠

She grabbed Bossy and me and her ran into the house. Her was yelling 📢 🆘 ‼️ , at daddy that we needed to get in the car and go to the emergency 🚗 vet ! ✂️ 🏥 💊 😨 🐕 daddy asked her how come and she said ....here it comes TMMI..... Bossy and I had purple poo, that's right PURPLE 💩

Daddy started laughing, him was laughing so hard he had tears 😂 😹
Mommy said "Stop laughing ! Stop laughing right now and help me" he kept laughing. I didn't feel sick 😐 😟 what was she talking about goin to the vet ??!, with daddy laughing 😂 😹 so hard, he was taking the attention off of us. I was hoping her would forget about the vet. I looked at 👀 Bossy and her looked 👀 at me, we both went to hide on our couch 🛋 under the blanket.

Mommy almost started crying 😢 she was frusturmerated wif daddy, he just kept laughing and laughing. Hims stood up and took
Mommy by the hand and hims said "honey, look..." hims pointed at our dinner plate 🍽 we had chicken and potatoes 🍗 🥔 . We had it for 3 nights along with our kibble. Yummy 😋 chicken 🍗 with purple potatoes 🥔 .

30

Yes, purple potatoes, remembers me telling you about mommy's purple potato salad ? Her had saved a few of the boiled potatoes for us. We love our taters. We don't get them a lot so when we do we savor da flavor of the taters.

I told you hers was bonkers.

Moral of the story ... if yous eat purple potatoes make sure your pawrents remember they fed em to yous. Thank you daddy for 'membering

Paws, kisses and purple
               Taters

~Monkey Mae

Monkey here !!!

I is in trouble again. I was jus trying to help mommy. Don't giggle ! 😊 It's true. 'Member me telling you guys about our cows 🐄 .... well mommy says dem attract flies and her is always chasing a fly or two around the house with a swatter. I felt a bad for her cuz her needed to start dinner but she was chasin da flyers. I climbed out of my monkey blanket and crept up on the back of the evil chair. I waited for the flyers to fly by me and I sprang into action ! I opened my monkey jaws and slurp !!! I got me a sky raisin ! Dems are deeeeeelicious 😋 😋 😋 😋
Mommy shrieked ! Hers said "No !!! No, Monkey Mae, you spit that out rights now !" Know what I did ? I looked her right in the eye 👁 and I chomped that yummy little sky raisin and swallowed hims whole !! Mommy turned green 🤢 her said "Monkey !! Flys are nasty !" True they aren't as yummy as cookies 🍪 , bully sticks or chicken jerky, but they come in a close 4th runner up ! Mommy said her needs to find Monkey mouthwash and I got a good teef scrubbing 🪥 then I showed her I climbed right up in her lap got into her face and I burped ! I didn't even say e'cuse me ! Her said no more cookies 🍪 for me today I need to learn to mind my manners. I bet once daddy gets home I get me a cookie 🍪 but for now I'll give mommy the evil eye from the comfort of my monkey blanket.

Paws, kisses and sky Raisins 🐾 🐾 ~Monkey Mae

Monkey here !!!

I gots to have company today !!! Who remembers the rascally babies ?, Ghost and Coffee Bean ? Ghost went to live with Sandy and Coffee Bean lives with his momma only his name isn't beanie anymores it's Toby now.

Toby's momma brought him and Miss Lucy over, mommy had to give Toby a shot !! I hates shots Mommy and Auntie Rhonda said hims had to get a shot so hims doesn't get sick
I was so so e'cited to see hims ! Hims r'membered all of us too ! We raced around the living room, we got to play outside even Bossy and Ol'e man Harley were happy to see him. (Probably because they knew Auntie Rhonda was taking him back home wif her)

Bossy and Harley were even nice to Miss Lucy. Can ya believe it ? Bossy was nice ... me either   DOH ! There mommy goes again "Monkey Mae mind yer manners " I is minding them, I telling the truth. We don't call her Bossy fer nothin.

That Toby, hims such a good boy. Mommy was gushing on and on abouts him cuz him stayed still and didn't cry one bit when hims got his shot.
Mommy tried to get good pictures of us playing but we were fast as lightning   and I definitely wasn't in the mood to cooperate. I was havin too much fun ! Hims remember'd where our food is and Hims helped himself and shocked his momma cuz Hims likes to pick at his food at home. Hims ran under the couch where I couldn't reach him and we played and played. Mommy said I was gonna sleep really well.

When Auntie Rhonda, Toby and Lucy left. Mommy had to finish sweeping and mopping. I crawled right onto my couch and under my monkey blanket. When mommy finished her chores her couldn't find me. Her looked high ⬆️⬇️➡️⬅️ and low her was calling my name. Her went out and got Uncle to help look 👀 for me. Uncle spotted me. Can you see me ?

I hope everyone is having a nice Saturday. I know I am. Maybe I'll get another cookie 🍪 later. Paws and kisses
🐾 💕 🐾
~Monkey Mae
Hide and go seek super star ⭐

Monkey here !!

I is da fabulous, supercalifragilisticexpidlidocious Monkey Mae!

I been practicing my dancing skills, I even let
Mommy put piggy 🐽 tails in my hair. I tried to gets daddy's attention but hims was making breakfast and it wasn't even for me. So I decided mommy wasn't so bad and I would get my attention from her.

But then ! Then ! I saw that evil 🐱 kitty cat. The one who invaded my monkey mansion. I been thinking and thinking 💭 about how to pay him back.

I rounded the troops, Harley was lookout 👀 hims was suppose to bark if mommy came. Bossy circled right, I circled left and bam 💥 I jumped right on his head !!

Harley didn't warn us, hims didn't sound the bark alarm 🔔 ! I thinks him wanted us to get in trouble. More cookies 🍪 for him.

Mommy came around the corner carrying a basket 🧺 full of laundry. That bad bad kitty 🐱 when I pounced on him hims jumped high into da
Air and hims screeched. Not cuz I hurted him, because hims wanted da Monkey Mae to gets in lots of trouble.

When hims screeched him scared mommy and that basket of clothes flew through the air ! 👕
👖 👚 🧦 👖 even the unmentionables. Whoops 😊 I just mentioned them 😶 that basket landed upside down on that bad kitty ! 🐱 hims was trapped like I was during my mansion invasion. I barked, Bossy barked and that kitty 🐱 was sitting there wif his eyes 👀 as big as saucers. I thinks I got my revenge.

Mommy had to pick up the laundry 🧺 but not before I grabbed a sock 🧦 and ran and hid under da Monkey blanket.

I think I earned myself a nap 😴 .

Love you all,
Paws and Kisses
🐾 💋 🐾

~ Monkey Mae

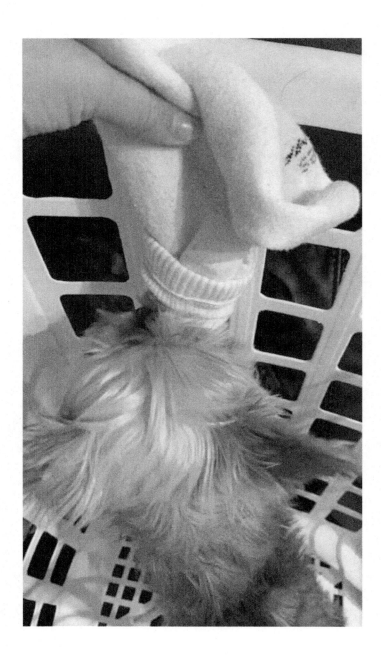

The horrors of being skunked in my Mhm's words

Let's take a moment and talk about Skunks.Let's take a moment and talk about Skunks.

My dogs were sprayed by a skunk lastnight I had let them out to potty and the fight was on, our large barn cat (20 pounds) jumped out from behind a large shrub and pounced on a skunk ! That's right a skunk! The dogs chased the cat who was chasing the skunk, I grabbed the puppy and ran for the door, the skunk was headed my way, the dogs passed the skunk and the cat was on the skunks tail, a fog of spray was washing over everything, dogs, cat, my porch, dogs yelping, cat squalling and a skunk hissing, me well I was screaming.....

I tend to use humor as a coping mechanism, as I sit here in my bed with eyes watering and simply believing I may have to replace my bedding, I truly am not sure I will be giving any of my 4 legged babies any snuggles anytime soon.

After a frantic and chaotic event such as this I was desperate to rid my fur babies of such a horrific smell. I sent my son to Walmart because I had seen a skunk shampoo in the pet section and because of the hour, I wasn't about to spend money on the emergency vet to bathe my dogs unless it was an actual medical emergency.

Which leads me to inform you of the horrors that unfolded after purchasing this "skunk" shampoo When my son arrived home I met him at the door and I think it's fair to say viciously ripped the de-skunk shampoo from his hands and attempted to bathe my dogs. The product boasts and I quote " Removes Skunk odor like nothing else on Earth." I would like to commend them for their honesty in advertising because it is true, it removes the skunk odor, although I think they should add a warning under that to include the following message ... BEWARE this product will assault your senses and quite possibly damage your sense of smell more so than the oily odor of the skunk.

The product when used as directed leaves you much worse off than just your dog reeking of skunk, my dogs and kitchen where I washed them now smell like skunk with a coverup of everything wrong and evil in the world, with a dash of citronella and coconut and a side of what I can only assume to be the flesh of some rotting road kill, although it is possible the lab created such a scent....which if it's lab created I would seek to fire every person working in their lab and start with a new stock of employees. And I don't recommend that as our economy really doesn't need more unemployed individuals. I'd like to suggest to them before marketing such a product, That each of their employees or anyone affiliated with their company be required to bathe their fur babies with this shampoo, regardless if they have been skunked or not, I strongly feel that they would immediately remove this product from manufacture and probably issue letters of apology to all involved.

I do understand that they offer a money back guarantee but I can't say the product failed in removing the smell of skunk, I just did not expect it to replace such odor with something so much more assaulting to the senses.

I admit my dogs are guilty of the original reason for needing the de-skunk shampoo but now the need for me to rub vapor rub under my nose and light every candle in my home and buy stock in Febreze is uncalled for, I just thought some would like to be made aware of the appalling situation.

Sincerely,

Jane Luman

Quite possibly wishing I suffered from hyposmia prior to use of your product

Have your babies been sprayed ? If so what did you use to get the scent off ? Also I do know it can be deadly and if they are sprayed in the eyes and the mouth you should rinse immediately with water and head to the veterinarian!!!

My dogs were sprayed by a skunk lastnight I had let them out to potty and the fight was on, our large barn cat (20 pounds) jumped out from behind a large shrub and pounced on a skunk ! That's right a skunk! The dogs chased the cat who was chasing the skunk, I grabbed the puppy and ran for the door, the skunk was headed my way, the dogs passed the skunk and the cat was on the skunks tail, a fog of spray was washing over everything, dogs, cat, my porch, dogs yelping, cat squalling and a skunk hissing, me well I was screaming.....

I tend to use humor as a coping mechanism, as I sit here in my bed with eyes watering and simply believing I may have to replace my bedding, I truly am not sure I will be giving any of my 4 legged babies any snuggles anytime soon.

After a frantic and chaotic event such as this I was desperate to rid my fur babies of such a horrific smell. I sent my son to Walmart because I had seen a skunk shampoo in the pet section and because of the hour, I wasn't about to spend money on the emergency vet to bathe my dogs unless it was an actual medical emergency.

Which leads me to inform you of the horrors that unfolded after purchasing this "skunk" shampoo When my son arrived home I met him at the door and I think it's fair to say viciously ripped the de-skunk shampoo from his hands and attempted to bathe my dogs. The product boasts and I quote " Removes Skunk odor like nothing else on Earth." I would like to commend them for their honesty in advertising because it is true, it removes the skunk odor, although I think they should add a warning under that to include the following message ... BEWARE this product will assault your senses and quite possibly damage your sense of smell more so than the oily odor of the skunk.

The product when used as directed leaves you much worse off than just your dog reeking of skunk, my dogs and kitchen where I washed them now smell like skunk with a coverup of everything wrong and evil in the world, with a dash of citronella and coconut and a side of what I can only assume to be the flesh of some rotting road kill, although it is possible the lab created such a scent....which if it's lab created I would seek to fire every person working in their lab and start with a new stock of employees. And I don't recommend that as our economy really doesn't need more unemployed individuals. I'd like to suggest to them before marketing such a product, That each of their employees or anyone affiliated with their company be required to bathe their fur babies with this shampoo, regardless if they have been skunked or not, I strongly feel that they would immediately remove this product from manufacture and probably issue letters of apology to all involved.

I do understand that they offer a money back guarantee but I can't say the product failed in removing the smell of skunk, I just did not expect it to replace such odor with something so much more assaulting to the senses.

I admit my dogs are guilty of the original reason for needing the de-skunk shampoo but now the need for me to rub vapor rub under my nose and light every candle in my home and buy stock in Febreze is uncalled for, I just thought some would like to be made aware of the appalling situation.

Sincerely,

Jane Luman

Quite possibly wishing I suffered from hyposmia prior to use of your product

Monkey here !!!

Mommy is mean ! Her is a mean mean mommy ! I gunna call her Meanie Head Mommy. MHM !

Hers bought us new bully sticks only dem aren't sticks. They are braided rings 🔘 ! What was her thinkin ?!?

I've tried tilting my head to the side to gnaw on it, I can't get a good grip. I tried standing on it, that didn't work. I even tried zipping around in circles to make it dizzy 😕 well I'm the one who got dizzy 😕

Bossy gave up. Her put hers on the big bed and crawled back on mommy's lap. Her said she doesn't have time to play wif her food.

Harley made mommy put him on the doggy couch 🛋 and hand him his ring 🔘. Hims over there gnawing away, I asked him how he got it and hims said he didn't know 🤔 What ?!? But hims is gnawing on it. He said it's all in the positioning . What da heck does that mean ?!?

I've tried the far side of the couch. No dice 🐒 I tried the middle seat 🐕 nada. I tried the third seat, zip. I tried the recliner, zero. I tried Daddy's chair, zilch !

Mommy is mean !! Her is a MHM ! Why is her torturing me ? Her knows I love Bully sticks ! This braided ring is Monkey torture! I demand an intervention!!!

I decided to try my luck on the couch again. I got into position. I turned that ring on it's end (hey rings don't have ends 😀)

Anyway, I placed one paw 🐾 inside the ring and held it still, or so I thought 💭. Leather is slippery and rings are rolly. That ring rolled and my paw 🐾 was inside 🔘 I dids the monkey splits ! I wasn't giving up. I used my sharp monkey teeth to hold it still and I clamped down on that ring !! And my teeth's held it !!! Ha ! I gots it ! No thanks to mommy, or should I say MHM.

Her thinks her is smart. I am smarter ! Her is still a meanie for making me work so hard on this bully ring. I hopes her buys the sticks, I heard her tells daddy that these rings last a long time and she thinks these are the ones she is going to buy from now on. I need to log onto her chewy account and make sure that doesn't happen. I'll show her ! We are gonna gets reoccurring monthly orders

Oh boy these bully rings are exhausting so I'm

Gonna take a nap on MHM's lap, but I still need an intervention! Less rings more sticks !!! Nap time is calling !

Paws and kisses

~ Monkey Mae the Sweet baby who needs an intervention from her Meanie head Mommy.

Monkey here!

I is in trouble. Big, big huge trouble. Like so much trouble I dunno if I'll ever get cookies again.

Mommy was carrying things to her go machine 🚙 and like a flash I was out the gate. I rans as fast as my monkey legs could carry me, up the gravel driveway and I turned left. I ran as fast as I could into the main moo moo pasture (🐄 🐄)
Right under the fence. Mommy was calling my name her was chasing after me. I showed her ! I slid right under that fence. Mommy had to go all the way up to the pasture gate. 😼

I saw them moo moo's and I started to chase them. I was barking my Monkey Mae head off. I just wanted to play with dem. All the moo moo's stopped what they were doing and just stared at me. 👀

Mommy had made it into the pasture and she was still running toward me. Then I saw a little moo I wanted to see it up close, I thinks it wanted to see me too cuz hims started coming toward me. The little Moo's mommy didn't look to happy. Maybe her was gonna have a talk with my mommy, and I don't think that would have been good for the little moo

Or this Monkey Mae.

I decided to tempt fate again and I circled to the right and ran-hell bent on having an adventure! ('Cuse my language)I stopped short when I saw the irrigation ditch.

Today is Thursday and water gets delivered down the ditch on Thursday ! I love water 💦 and, I'm sure you know what that means ! Yep yep I decided it would be a grand idea to take a swim in that ditch. Mommy caught me right as I was about to jump. I knew right away I was in big big trouble.

47

The look on mommy's face I knew I had scared her. She carried me all the way back to the pasture gate I dunno why she didn't go under the fence like I did, it's much faster than walking all that way 🙈 I decided I should tell Mommy I'm sorry so I snuggled up to her neck and held onto her shoulder. I thinks her is still mad at me. Her said her isn't mad, but that I just scared her.

When we gots in the house, her called my daddy and tattle-tailed on me ! Her kept saying she was glad the Bull got moved to the far pasture. Can you believe it ? How embarrassing. Now I gotta be extra sweet to daddy when hims gets home. He will forgive me cuz I gots him wrapped around my paw 🐾 I bets I even get him to gimme a cookie 🍪

Well I better go give my
Mommy some paws and kisses.
Sending you all paws and kisses too

🐾🐾🐾

~ Monkey Mae
Moo moo wrangler 🐄 🐵

> **WISHING I HAD COWBOY BOOTS**
>
> **MAYBE I COULD HAVE OUT RUN MOMMY**

Monkey here !

I don'ts know what is going on here in my house, but it not ok. Not ok at all !!

I tells you a secret 😊 I likes to sneak into the back room and eat kitty 🐱 food. It's yummy 😋 it has chicken pieces in it.

This morning I come back from outside and you knows what ?!? Mommy put a gate up across the dining room so now I can't get into the back room 😢

Those kitty's jus jump right over and they get to go eat their food, and here I sit a sad little Monkey Mae because I can'ts eat their food too.

I protest, this is not ok. I da Monkey Mae and ifs I want to snack on da kitty 🐱 food I will ! Well not now cuz MHM put a gate up, her says it's to keep Monkey's out ! That is not fair ! I do not like that !

I decided I would wait for the perfect opportunity to present itself and I, da Monkey Mae would make my move. I would gets me some of those tasty 😋 🐱 kitty morsels.

MHM already had one strike against her because of that darn gate, but then hers hada go to the store and her lefted us at home wif our hooman brother. Strike 2 MHM ! Although it did gimme time to think 🤔 and come up with a plan on how to get me some tasty 😋 🐱 kitty morsels.

When MHM got home 🏠 her and brother unloaded the go machine 🚙 she triple checked the gate to the yard, guess hers didn't wanna run today 🐱

They were bringing lots of bags in the house and setting them all over the table and the counters, my brother put one bag on the floor 🐱 it was a good bag too! It hads carrots 🥕, and apples 🍎 and peaches 🍑 in it. I love dem things ! I loves thems a lot ! 😋 😊 I sniffed me out, I knew dems yummy carrots 🥕 apples 🍎 and peaches 🍑 were in that bag !, I hada get me some. MHM went to get the last of the bags out of the go machine 🚗 and I made my move ! I gots right into that bag and I got a bite of everything. MHM came around the corner and caught me munching on carrots 🥕

(Don't worry mommy checked the bag and I didn't eat any plastic I just used my teeth 🦷 and paws 🐾 to open it)

I made the executive decision to eats my fruits and veggies so I can gets over that gate and get to those delicious 😋 kitty 🐱 morsels.

Paws and kisses

🐾 💋 🐾

~ Monkey Mae
Da' girl who eats her fruits and veggies

Monkey here !

I wants to talk about last night.
Mommy said "Goodnight Monkey Mae" and her gave me my chicken jerky and put me in da Monkey Mae Mansion. I ate my jerky. I wasn't ready to go to sleep 😴.

I had to rearrange my whole mansion. Mommy washed my blankets and her messed dem all up. Her destroyed my blanket nest. That just wouldn't do for sleeping purposes. First, I used my paws 🐾 and I dug and dug until the top blanket was unfolded and all messy. Then I took da bottom blanket in my teeth 🦷 and shook it. The whole mansion was shaking, I caused a Monkey Mae Earth 🌍 shake ! I heards a voice in da dark say "Monkey Mae, you stop all dat shakin it's night night time" .... Says who ? I, da Monkey Mae and i's can't see you 🙈 I circled in and around, over and under my blankets. I made a little fort 🏰 I crawled in and settled down for a rest.

What was dat ??? I heards a noise outside !! ⏰ Da Monkey Mae alarm
System was going off. I growled my bestest fiercest growl. A real good one, low and mean like Miss Bossy taught me. Den what do I hear ? My daddy, him told me, "Monkey Mae, it's ok be quiet it's bedtime" it was

most certainly NOT ok I heards sumthin !!

Next, I gave my best Monkey Mae bark. 2 sharp high pitched Yips ! Mommy was not happy. Her said "That's enough !, Monkey. Do you hear me, you need to be quiet 👻 " Of course I hear her, I not deaf. I do not have selective hearing like her ! Her picks and chooses what her wants to hear. Mostly she has it when's I am telling her I need more cookies 🍪

I settled back into my nest, closed my eyes and took a little nap. I heard a crash outside ! Sound the alarm 🚨 !!! I opened up my lungs and let loose ! I barked and barked and barked ! Mommy said "Monkey Mae stop barking your fool head off !, that is enough !" I answered her with more barks ! This was an emergency something crashed outside ! Mommy says "Monkey Mae it is 2:30 am 🕝 it is time for sleeping not barking , that's enough now. That is the wind 💨 through the trees 🌳 " I never heards the wind do that noise.

I needed to stay alert to warn everyone if I heards anything else. Harley couldn't hear nuthin hims was buried under the covers. Bossy?, well her had her paws 🐾 over her head and was snoring 😴 . Neither of them were any help at all. This was a job for da Monkey Mae !

Tap, tap, tap, drip,drop,drip I heards water 💧 falling !!! Wake up wake up wake uppppp!!!! It's dark and I wanna go swimming in the moonlight 🌙 Ut oh here comes daddy. Him opened the mansion door and lets me out. I barked and barked tryin to tell him I wanted to go swimming. He picked me up and puts me in da big bed. Him said "Settle down Monk, it's da rain 🌧 outside and da wind 💨 . Now go to sleep. But I, da Monkey Mae had other ideas 💡

I raced around the big bed, dove under da pillows. Raced across mommy. Jumped on a lump under da covers that was Harley. He didn't like that. I stepped on Bossy's nose. Her growled at me. I raced across daddy's face. Him wasn't very happy. Mommy said that wasn't the way to behave at 3:06 am 🕒

54

Daddy tried rubbing my belly to calm me. That wasn't happening! I chewed on his fingers. I got tangled in mommy's hair. I kept up my hot laps around the bed. If I wasn't sleepy I wasn't gonna let anyone else sleep 😾 eithers.

At 4:45 am I let my daddy sleep for 15 minutes until his alarm ⏰ went off for him to get ready for work 🥱 👕 👖 👟 And you know what hims did ?!? Hims disturbed me ! I was trying to sleep and hims wasn't letting me ! Mommy made me gets out of da big bed too. She kept poking me while she was drinking her coffee ☕ her said if I didn't let her sleep her wasn't gonna let me sleep either. Mommy is cranky. Her is a MHM. I needs my beauty sleep 😾 It's hard to be this cute. Her better watch out or I'll keep her up all night again 😼

But hers really gotta stop pokin me. I thinks I'll go in my mansion and have myself a good Monkey Mae nap 💤 now I just gotta get in there without being caught. 👀 I need some luck 🍀 I thinks I gonna win.

Paws and kisses

🐾 💜 🐾

~Monkey Mae

An ornery little girl who likes to deprive her mommy and daddy of sleep.

Monkey here !

I love sunny ☀ days. I like to run in the grass and sniff the flowers 🌼. If I'm lucky I find all kinds of creepy crawlies...bugs 🐛 and flyers 🦋
I likes to roll in the grass and feel da sun on my belly.

MHM says I have to warn you before reading 📖 today. Like that warning they put in movies 🎥 So here goes : Butterflies 🦋 were harmed !

There hasn't been a lot to do 'round here. MHM has been cranky. The power company has turned our power off as a "safety"measure, daddy says it's because of where we live and all the wildfires. MHM isn't happy cuz hers has to wash da dishes by carryin in water,We have a well we can't get water if we don't gots power, and her is tired of making dinners on da stovetop instead of being able to cook in da oven ... MHM is cranky.

Anyway we been spending lots of time outside before it gets too hot 😓

Harley just sunbathes. Him lays in da middle of da walkway and shows his business to everyone. 🐢 Dat is not sumethin I wants ta see !

Bossy, her uses the ramp to get to the yard now instead of the stairs cuz hers belly is getting big an her walks like a duck 🦆
"Monkey Mae !!"
👀 Ut oh .....
"Monkey Mae, if we can't say something nice, we don't say anything at all"

See I tolds you her is being a MHM. I was jus telling da truths about Bossy's belly.

Anyway back to Me !! I da Monkey Mae, explorer of the yard ! I likes to
Watch da hummingbirds who come to eat outa the feeders mommy and daddy fill for them. I like it when they dive bomb 🐦 da kitty 🐱 hims doesn't like it but hims deserves it cuz hims invaded my monkey mansion.

Today, I was minding my own business. "WHAT "? I really was 🦋 I dunno 🐵 why dats so hard for you all to believe. I rounded da corner of the house where mommy has a lot of planter boxes. And I saws them !!! Butterflies 🦋! Mommy calls dem moths (Hahncappsia moth) thems like to land on da lawn I sneaked up on them. I crouched low in da grass and I crept forward very very slowly. It was really hard for me ta do cuz I was excited to see da flutterflies. 🦋 I gots close e'ough to pounce !!!

Dat flutterfly flew up and landed on my head ! It tickled ! I ran in a circle it flew away but as I ran about 10 more flutterflies flew up out of da grass ! Jackpot !!! 🎰

I was so e'cited ! I lept in da air and I caughts me a flutterfly !! I caughts it in my Monkey Mae mouth ! Phew! It tasted icky ! I spits him out. Den 3 of them flutterflies were circling my head ! I jumped up and caughts me another one ! I spits it out fast 🦋 cuz dems taste icky! I stepped on it with my feet's 🐾 It was tickling my paws 🐾 wif it's wings 🦋 I was so excited 😊 den.... I dunno what came over me. I nipped da flutterfly. Dems other flutterflies were divebombing my head ! I just couldn't help myself. That's when it happened. I got to rough and I smooshed da flutterfly. 🐾🦋🐾 😞

Mommy wasn't mad at me. Hers just said dat I gots to be more careful that those are fragile creatures. I think I need to find something a little tougher to play wif me....
AHHHH ! There's da Kitty 🐱 I gots a friend !

Paws and kisses
🐾 💋 🐾
~ Monkey Mae
Defender of da yard !

Monkey here !

Sumthin strange is going on and I can't put my paw 🐾 on it.

We gots our power back on after 3 long days so mommy has lots to do around da house. Her has left me to entertain myself her kept saying "oh boy, I hope you behave Monkey"

Hmmmpt !! I always behave 😺 I don'ts know what her is talkin bout, do you ?!?!

Harley is loving this power thing. Hims is sleepin 😴 under da blankets hims is like mommy her loves to sleep when it's cold 😊 So hims has been catching up on his sleeps.

But here is the ringer ! The thing I can't put my paw 🐾 on.

Bossy has been so nice to me ! Her has curled up wif me to nap 💤. Her has given me kisses 😘. Her has even shared her bully stick !! I love dem sticks ! I dunno what's goin on, but I think 🤔 I likes it.

Mommy says that Bossy gets into momma mode and loves on everyone more than usual. Heck if this is what happens I'll take it !! Hers is gonna be a great momma. I bets since she is liking me so much her will let me play wif da babies when dem gets here.

I thinks 🍪 that I gonna share my cookies 🍪 wif Bossy this afternoon, I won't let mommy forget cookies 🍪 even if hers is still busy. But for now we will snuggle up and have a nap 😴 together.

Paws and Kisses - Monkey Mae

Monkey here !

Betcha all thought I ran away or dat my mommy locked 🔒 me up and threwed away da key 🔑 well I didn't run away, and her didn't lock me up. Her has just been busy with her dad and my hooman brother.

My hooman brother got to go to his grandma's house. Her took him to a punkin farm 🎃 They only had a few minutes to look 👀 around and his granny told him "Ryan, I know you want a pumpkin, I want you to pick the first one that speaks to you"

I think Grandma is as crazy as mommy, pumpkins don't speak ! What is her talking 'bout ? Well Ryan found him the first punkin that spoke

to him, that's what he told his granny. I bet you a dollar 💵 that granny about spit her tea out when her saw the punkin that "spoke" to Ryan. And I betcha her thought her grandson would get a hernia tryin to put it in da go machine 🚗

Ryan's sister brought him home 🏠 and her told

Mommy, about dis pumpkin 🎃 her said and I quote "Mom, wait until you see the pumpkin granny got Ryan. He needs help getting it out of the car. I think it's the biggest pumpkin I've ever seen." Mommy rolled her eyes because Maddy exaggerates a lot and then mommy said " 🙄 😲 " 👀 I is a lady so I can't say those words and I don't like soap 🧼 in my mouth so I refuse to repeat what mommy said. I thinks hers was shocked 😲 it was that big.

Luckily Ryan didn't get a hernia he was able to get his punkin right inside the gate into our yard. I hope you enjoy my great pumpkin pictures.

Paws and Kisses

Monkey Mae

Queen 👑 of the giant Pumpkin 🎃

ITS THE GREAT PUMPKIN CHARLIE BROWN !!!

Monkey here !!

This is Monkey abuse !!

Yesterday was awful jus mighta have been the worst day of my Monkey Mae life ! Pure Monkey abuse I tells ya !

First mommy has me in a ridiculous diaper. And den Mommy shoved

A nasty 😣 pill down my throat so her could take me in da go machine 🚙 well I showed her and I spit it out all

Over daddy on his side of da bed 🐱 and mommy hada scoop up dat soggy pill and try to give it to me YUCK !!!! But guess what I still got car sick 🤢 her took me to see Dr. D

Him looked 👀 at my ears because mommy said they were red and that I was scratching at them. He agreed wif her and said that they were inflamed and him gave her some drops 💧 I don't like dem !!! Hims also said that my cough is from allergies and I needs a pill 💊 for da mucus in my throat !!! I do not like pills ! I bite mommy ! I bite her hard when her tries to give me pills 💊 hims gave her 5 pills to give me anyway !!! I am not happy at all ! That is Monkey abuse ! Then ! Then him gave me a shot ! 💉 I didn't mind that much, because shots don't bother me, but don't even think about mentioning pills 💊 around me ! That is grounds for filing charges of abuse! Abuse I tell you !!!

Then mommy had to take her to machine where all the go

Machines go to get tuned up and while we waited with all the other people I saw a really small person. Mommy said it was a baby. Him was really cute. He screamed, I barked. He clapped, I wagged my tail. I wanted to play with him, but mommy said he was too little to play with. 😊 his mommy let him touch me, he was really gentle. I think I like babies. He wears diapers too, so now I'm not as embarrassed wearing mine. Finally we were done waiting on mommy's go machine and we headed off to go

Meet aunt Cyndi cuz her had some better diapers she said mommy could have for me. (Thank goodness cuz these things mommy had me in were fer the birds 🐦)

We met Aunt Cyndi at her nail appointment where her was getting spooky nails. I bought my grandma Shelby a Halloween dress to thank Auntie for my new diapers her was giving me. They are really nice. Mommy got us home and it was still dark. Cuz PG&E still had us in da public safety power shut off by the way that's not what mommy calls it 😕 😩 😡 her said 4 days was long enough this time and her was tired of living with da generator. She said there's only so many camping and generator jokes she can make until it just isn't funny anymore. But we are blessed because power was restored at 7:00pm last night.

But back to the abuse... her put my pill in my favorite thing .... cheese 🧀 her tricked me !!! I took my pill without a fuss !!! No muss !!! I da Monkey Mae, Pill hater, pill spitter outer, alligator teeth, mommy biter, pill refuser , cheese lover 🧀 ATE THAT PILL !! Monkey Mae abuse !!! This is a travesty! That's it ! This is the final straw I tell you ! I am now taking applications for a new home. If you meet the following requirements please submit an application.

1. Must feed me bully sticks not rings

2. No cats

3. Socks

4. No diapers

5. Cheese

6. My own mansion

7. Fenced yard with flutterflies

8. blue buffalo training treats

9. Chicken jerky(must be homemade)

10. Tutu's

11. No pills of any kind ever no matter what no exemptions nope not ever

12. Sing me lullabies and rub my belly to put me to sleep at bedtime just like my daddy does

13 allow me to add to this list at any time because I am da Monkey Mae and I can never make up my mind completely and it is always subject to change

Paws and kisses

Poor abused

Monkey Mae

Monkey here !

I might have kinda sorta been in a wee bit of trouble lately. Yes, me. I know dat's very hard to believe isn't it ? I, the perfectly well behaved wonderful Monkey Mae 😇 .

Here's what is happening. I like to be the center of attention. Not just a tiny bit but a WHOLE lot a bit. Well dat Bossy her is gettin lots of attentions lots of belly rubs MORE den ME !!! and her is getting special loves 💕 Mommy picks her up and puts her on da chair and off da chair and on da couch and off da couch and on da bed and off da bed. It just isn't fair ! Mommy only puts me on and off da bed ! Her says I am too fast 🙄 and I leap on and off the couch and chair 'fore her can catch me. I say her is making 'cuses again.

So I decided at bed time when I went into my Monkey mansion with all

My snuggly blankies and babies and my chicken jerky. I was gonna gobble up my jerky and den... den... I was gonna lay in wait. I was gonna carefully and quietly 😊 wait until I heard daddy snoring 😼 and when I knew mommy had found her comfy spot and her was almost asleep. DEN ! I was gonna make my move of attack ! First I made my cute little Monkey Mae moan, just to remind mommy I was in my mansion(like her didn't already know that, her locked me in there, her probably threw away da key 🔑 too 😒) mommy said "Oh hush 🤫 Monk, it's time for bed"

It most certainly was not time for bed !, it was only phase one of my attack!

Next I let out 3 sharp barks! BARK!BARK!BARK!

This time it was daddy, he is much nicer than MHM, he said "oh baby girl what's wrong are you cold, lock momma I think she's cold." I wasn't cold at all I had my 3 best snuggly blankies in there but I did my best fake shiver 😬

Mommy sighed the sigh she does when she is really annoyed the one she reserves for the other hooman brother and his girlfriend when he asks to brings her to dinner 🙄 (this was getting somewhere, phase 2 was complete)

I laid down, I let them get comfy in their bed again, daddy started snoring 💤 and phase 3. I started barking my fool head off. I barked as if the boogie man was after me. 👻 I barked like the mailman was in the front yard. ✉️ I barked like there was a squirrel 🐿️ in the living room. I barked for the sake of barking and nothing could stop me. Not one single thing.

Not. One. Single. Thing. ...... except. ...... well thinking 🤔 I did have a motive in all of this and that was to gain access to the hooman bed. I wanted to sleep with daddy. Not MHM.

Then like music 🎵 to my Monkey Mae ears what do I hear ???

Daddy to the rescue he tells mommy to let me out and get my monkey blanket and put me in bed next to him !!! Hahaha MHM I won !

Thanks daddy we will

Sleep good now. Too bad for MHM. So what if she has 3 Yorkies on her side of the bed 🙈 we are small and we don't take up that much room.... or do we ? 😼

Paws and kisses

🐾 😺 of the king size bed Monkey Mae

Monkey here !

It's been a while, MHM has been busy wif da new babies and Miss Bossy. We also have been dealing wif the lovely power outages because we live in California. Well since MHM has been so busy she has been walking around in zombie 🧟 mode and no it isn't because today is Halloween 💀 . Her has been at Miss Bossy's beck and call. Her even cuts up liver for her. Her has cooked her scrambled eggs. Bought her all different kinds of food, even tried feedin her special homemade Dog food. I thinks Miss Bossy is foolin MHM and pullin da wool over her eyes. MHM is fallin for it too ! M 🙄 This is getting out of paws 🐾 I tell you simply out of paws. Someone needs to sit MHM down and have a talk wif her. Sure dem babies are cute, and yes Miss Bossy did a good job, and yeah we all wanna kiss their noses, but pfffft! Enough all ready! Turn the electricity on and let's get the show on da road people ! I, is da Monkey Mae ! I needs some attention ! I deserve some attention! It is simply not enough that I now rule the entire king size bed while Miss Bossy and her crew of babies sleep in a special crate next to MHM on da floor.

If Miss Bossy makes a sound or those babies make Sounds that mommy doesn't like there her goes bangin around in da dark gettin a flashlight 🔦 and wakin me up ! 👀 I needs my beauty sleeps ! I is da Monkey Mae ! I demand sleeps ! Who does her think she is ? That rotten ol' MHM. It was muggy in da bedroom, we couldn't have da window open for any fresh air ya wanna know why ? I tell ya . Because of those babies !! Dats why ! Dey can't get cold. So here I am overheated and miserable. Quite frankly this was no way to get a good nights rest. Crash ! 💥 MHM has that blasted flashlight 🔦 again ! Dagnabbit ! What was her trying to do to me ! I want my sleep ! Baby check complete.

Looks like MHM was settling down again. Maybe she was going to sleep this time. It's hot 😓 I cannot get comfortable, I was tossing and turning. From top of the bed to the bottom of the bed, from By daddy's head to the crook in MHM's leg.... wait a minute....

I spy 🔍 with my little Monkey Mae eye 👁 ..... MHM had her foot 🦶 peeking out from under the covers. 😏 I couldn't resist. I snuck closer. I stuck my little tongue 👅 out and I licked MHM on the toe .She moved a bit. Oh this was sort of fun. I tried my luck again. Lick 👅 Mommy jerked her foot 🦶 a little harder that time. Hmmm 🤔 this was kinda fun. Time to pay MHM back for these sleepless nights and being blinded by flashlights 🔦 . Slurrrrrrrrrp I gave a good lick 👅 that time. MHM jumped she half sat up ! She almost kicked me off the bed ! Me ! Da Monkey Mae ! I almost went a flying ! That was not good ! Her wasn't even awake ! Her was sleep 💤 movin. This wasn't ok. Her was so tired. Her didn't even realize that she sat up sleeping? What da heck is wrong wif her ? It wasn't time to fly it was time to Sleep 💤 not send me flying. Hmmmpft ! I'll Show her !

She laid back down.... foot 🦶 sticking out of da blankets again. I was a little miffed MHM her had tried to send me flyin so I knew I had to teach her a lesson her deserved a lesson, her needed to learn something from the flashlights 🔦 and catering to someone other than ME, the fantastic, wonderful, stupendous, Monkey Mae. Yep it was lesson time for MHM.!!Sure licking her toe 🦶 was interesting but I had a better plan. I opened up my Monkey Mae mouth and chomped down on MHM's toe 🦶 ! She sat up that time alright ! Wide awake ! Eyes open ! 👀 sure she was tired, even delirious from lack of sleep 💤 In fact her didn't even fully wake up !! And the next morning she only remembered about my 🦶 toe biting because she saw her little toe had small red bite marks on it. 🐾 ✋ guilty as charged. 🐵 It was me. I did that. Me, da Monkey Mae. Biter of MHM' baby toe.... hehehe 😏 I bet MHM learned her lesson. And doesn't sleep wif her feet pokin out of da covers again when her is sleep deprived.

Sending lots of love.
 And don't bite your mommy or daddy's toes unless they try ta send ya flyin !

🐾 🐾 🐾
Monkey Mae

Monkey here !

So raise your paws 🐾 if dis whole time you been duped inta thinkin TOT was for Tongue out Tuesday cuz our mommy's and daddy's try to take our pictures 📷 of us by tricking us with yummy snacks an other things, ta get us to stick our tongues 👅 out ! BUT !! BUT ! If we sticks our tongues out any other time we will get in big troubles ! Pfffft ! Double standards I tell ya. Dem hoomans are crazy.

So last night I should have known something was goin on. MHM was way to nice to me. She went around picking up all the food bowls and water bowls before bedtime 🛏 ..... den her gave me not jus 1 chicken jerky but 2 !!! And I got them early too 🍗 !!! Den her put up dat blasted puppy gate dat her uses to keep me out of da room where da kitty 🐱 food is at, cuz well I may or may not have learned how to get on da computer chair, den jump to da sitting chair and from dat chair over to da guest bed 🛏 and from dat I may or may not be able to reach the little table that the kitty food sits on 🥣 .... So I shoulda know her had somethin up her sleeve 😏

Den ! Dis morning 🌙 when it was still dark outside her got me out of bed 🛏 ! I was warm and snuggly next to my daddy ! That is a punishable offense! 🚔 👮 🚨
Her forced me outside and made me go potty it was cold too ! Den when I came inside der wasn't anythin for me to eat or drink !!!
I had a moment of relieve when her put me back in bed wif my daddy. I heard her putting da food and water down. Whew 😌 what a relief! Her wasn't starving us ! She wasn't ! I knew daddy wouldn't let her do dat not to da Monkey Mae ! Nope nope !
Den ! Den her came back. AND KNOW WHAT HER DID NEXT ??? MHM took me and put me in da go machine 🚗 and off we went ! We went to da vet ! To Dr. Darling !!

This time was different something wasn't right. I couldn't put my paws 🐾 on it. Da girls all said Hello Monkey Mae, and Jasmine gave me hugs and held me. That was fine, I didn't want MHM holding me, her was a trickster. Taking food and water away, waking me up early and taking me out of bed ! then taking me in da go machine ! What I heard next left me wondering if I needed a hearing test. Jasmine said "Come with me Monkey Mae we will see mommy later" wait... what !?

So as it turns out TOT is not Tongue Out Tuesday!! 🦷 It just so happens that this TOT is Teef Out Tuesday for Monkey Mae !

MHM says I will get a visit from the Teef fairy 🧚 I do not even know what a Teef fairy 🧚 is. Her says it's a magical fairy 🧚 dat brings treats. Well I likes bully sticks but my mouth hurts too bad to even think about those ! I told her I is gonna tell all my friends about what her did to me and her said that it had to be done, because I couldn't keep all my baby teefs and my big girl teefs too. I said sure I could da more da merrier ! Her said dat simply wasn't true and that I needed the surgery to make sure I stayed healthy. I'm still upset wif her. Her said I will feel a lot better in a few days, but for now I'm pouting and sticking close to daddy.

Just paws 🐾 today.
Lots of love 💕
Monkey Mae

Souvenir ?

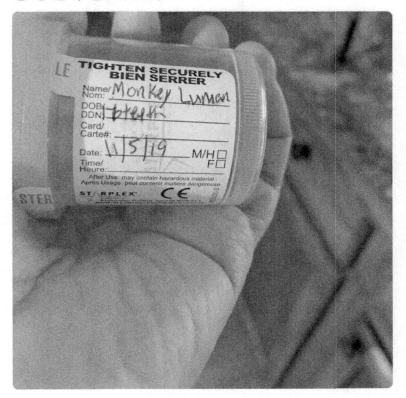

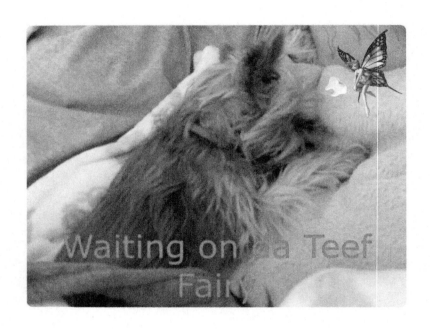

Monkey here !!

Hi guys. I gots a confession ta make. It actually got cold 😅 last night. Probably not as cold as some of you get but it was cold for da Monkey Mae.

When it was bedtime 🛏 ya wanna know what's I did ? Well I gunna tell yous. I let daddy love 💕 on me a little bit but I wasn't too interested in getting cuddles, not from daddy. Miss Bossy was sleepin by MHM and Mr. Old man Harley was at her feets. 🐾

Daddy took my monkey blanket and hims made me a little nest right next to him where I always sleep 😴. I didn't want to act ungrateful so I laid on it for ohhh probably 15 seconds. ⏰ Den, I was on da move. I crept up outa my nest, I looked 👀 to see if hims was watching. Him wasn't.... I was safe. I crept a little further, an a little further. Till I was free from da Monkey nest. Den.... I mades my move. I very carefully moved over to MHM, oh her smells good. Her was still warm from usin da blow machine to dry her hair after her shower 🚿 I dunno why you hoomans like dat thing. It makes too much noise I know I don't like it when Miss Denise does my hairs. 🙀 Anyhoo... MHM smelled goods it reminded me when I was tiny and her first took me home, and her was warm !! I crept right up to her. Her and daddy were watching TV 📺 Her had her right arm propped up under her head. I couldn't believe my eyes! 👀 da whole right side of MHM was warm and cozy and it was all for da Monkey Mae !!! I crawled right up, did 3 turns and laid down. 💤 I kicked a few times, den I stretcheddddd all da way out. Mhm laughed 😊 and said "Monkey Mae, what are you doing" ? Hmmm 😜 what's it look like I is tryin to go Ni Ni, I scooted my body till my head was right under MHM's armpit whew 😌 good things her smelled good huh !? 😊 den I stretched my back legs all da way down, I flipped my tail a few times too, till it was straight out. My front paws 🐾 I sorta felt like I abandoned daddy so I stretched them towards him. I wanted da best of both worlds. 🌍 I had a plan I'd sleep next to MHM but I'd touch daddy so him didn't get hims feelers hurt . 😊 My plan worked !! Daddy reached over and started givin me a front paw 🐾 massage. Oooh 😊 I love dat. Ni Ni Monkey Mae. 💤 😴 🛏

It was so warm and snuggly. Da only bad part is MHM gets up a lot !! Her checks on da babies all night long. I didn't want her ta get back in bed and her spot be cold 🥶 so every time her would get up I'd scootch over and lay wif my head on her pillow, and my body where her sleeps. Jus tryin to do my part.

So my confession is, I abandoned daddy last night. I needed some MHM time. Her isn't a MHM today. Her is a pretty good mommy, I enjoyed my mommy time last night. So far her isn't too bad today either.... her let me play wif da babies !!! I LOVE da babies !! 🐾 🐾 🐾 🐾

Gotta run da babies wanna play some more !

Paws and kisses
🐾💕🐾
Monkey Mae best baby sitter ever ! And MHM snuggler... on my terms 😉

Good Morning Monkey here !!!

Today MHM is cranky. Her needs lots of coffee ☕ . I only has a little bit of blame on her bein cranky pants 👢

Daddy gave us all a rib bone yesterday from the Prime Rib he cooked on Christmas 🎄 (Don't worry 😊 mommy just lets us chew the marrow out, Dr. Darling said it was safe with supervision) 🐕 🐕

We were in heaven ! It was so yummy 😋 we chewed and chewed. Till our jaws hurt. Ol'e man even fell asleep on the floor wif his bone 🦴 Bossy and I shared, her would switch bones 🦴 wif me and we would chew and chew some more. We got tired too, that's a lot of work !

It was time for bed and MHM settled us in. Harley crawled under da blankets by MHM's feets 🦶 Bossy sleeps in between MHM and daddy, her lays by MHM's hip. Me ? Da super fabulous, beautiful, silly Monkey Mae ? Well I have a special spot. Daddy makes me my own blanket bed, up by da headboard on my own monkey 🐵 blanket wif a super soft gray blankie he uses to tuck me in . 💤

I took a nap 😴 and den at 3 o'clock I decided I needed my bone. I tried to wake up MHM by staring 👀 at her. Dat didn't work. 😾 I walked down the bed stopping at Bossy and gave her a few sniffs 👃 I moved on to Harley, I stuck my head under da blankets and Hims growled at me ! Ol'e grumpy man.

82

MHM said "Monkey Mae dats enough, go back to bed " Hmmmpt. MHM still wasn't paying enough attention to me ! Dis was important! I needed dat Bone ! I walked back up to my blankie bed I really thought about going back to sleep I promise I did. Dat Bone was on my mind. So I made my move, I jumped right on MHM's head ! Den I ran down her body as fast as I could ! Her shot up like a rocket ! I was too fast her reached for me but didn't get me, so I sat at the bottom of da bed and I tried to tell her ! I yipped, I growled, I even barked at her. Daddy said "
Better take her out, she might need to potty "

I most certainly did not need to potty but !, if MHM got outs of bed I was 1 step closer to my bone ! MHM got up, her gots her slippers on den her robe, she opened da bedroom Door and like a flash I was out of dere ! I got to my bone in record time and here came MHM ! her scooped me up and took me outside! What was her thinkin !?! It was 3:30 it wasn't outside time, it was Monkey Mae bone gnawing time !!
Her let me back in and boom I was after dat bone ! MHM scooped me up again and forced me back to bed ! I was not happy !, not even a little bit. I wasn't going back to sleep ! Her couldn't make me ! I raced up her body I did hot laps at her feets, and repeat ! Up and down, round and round. MHM tried to put me in bed, her rubbed my belly (oooooh I loves dat   ) I wasn't giving in, dat bone was too important ! MHM wasn't listening ! I'd show her !, I'd have daddy help me ! I jumped onto daddy !, right on his head ! Him said " Monkey ! Dats enough !!" Him used his serious voice he put me back in my bed and Hims loved on me. I gave up and wents back to sleep, I don't like daddy's serious voice. MHM and daddy had trouble going back to sleeps, them tossed and turned until after 6 am, didn't dey know they were disturbing my beauty sleeps .
Dis morning MHM got out of bed to make coffee and I ran out to da living room. I raced to where I left my bone and you know what ?!? DO YA ? my bone was gone ! I raced to where Bossy left her bone it was gone ! I flew across the living room to Harley's hiding place and his was gone too !!! MHM had stolen our bones and her threw them away !!
Her is sitting her sippin coffee and now I'm going to take a nap, I not going to sit by her, I am gonna ignore her for stealin my bones her is a MHM today and her is gonna learn dat her is in big trouble! Her is grounded ! ...... oh wait her has a bully stick ! Gotta go !

Love paws and bones
Monkey Mae

Helloooo it's me Monkey Mae !!

I is sorry I haven't been around much, lots has been going on. I wanna share my adventures wif you guys.

We wents to da Okie-homa. 🌎 Dat is where I was born before mommy and daddy brought me to live wif dem. First we had to gets up at 3 in da morning ⏰ so Mommy could give me my travel medicine 💊 den we had to get in da go-machine 🚗 to go to da aeroport ✈️ .

We went in a line and mommy took her shoes 👟 off an puts dem in a bin, den her put her purse 👜 in a bin and DEN !!?, her puts my Monkey bag 🎒 in a bin. "Hey hey guys, dat bag had my blankie, my treats, my kibble. 🦴 All da important Monkey Mae survival kit stuffs. Mommy helded me an we had to walk in a weird contraption. Den some man wiped mommy's hands wif somethin. He told mommy not ta move till hims said it was ok. Her stayed still, I always move when someone tells me not to. 🐒 Den we got to get our stuff out of da bin. we walked to another long line and got on da plane ✈️ Mommy said we had to ride in 2 planes ✈️ we flew from Sacramento to Dallas Texas first. Oh man do ya know Dey don't gots a yard on da plane ? Did ya know you gotta stay seated wif your seat 💺 belt fastened ? Oh man I had to go potty 🚽 real bad ! When we landed mommy put my socks 🧦 on her said it was to protect my feet's from germs 🦠 her let me walk on my leash. I was so excited to see all those different peoples. Peoples stopped and wanted to pet me. I let them ! But boy oh boy I still needed a potty.

85

Mommy and daddy found a pet relief area. It had a red fire hydrant, a hose, poop 💩 bags and green turf grass. This was not a yard. It smelled funny. I don't like the turf grass. So I refused to potty 💦 in there. Off we went to the other gate to wait for our plane ✈️ I dunno if any of yous have been to DFW aeroport but lemme tell you it isn't small. We landed at Terminal A we had to go to Terminal D. It's so big Dey even have an E terminal 👀 !!! We rode a skylink. It goes fast 💨 we gots to terminal D and mommy and daddy wanted to eat something, we walked and walked and walked 😩 I was stopping traffic left and right everyone loved me 🐾 🐾 🐾 Den somethin awful happened. I couldn't wait anymore ! I decided the middle of DFW was a perfect place to leave a Monkey Mae memory. 💩 I've never seen Mommy move so fast. Her scooped da poop 💩 into a poop bag 💩 and pulled out a baby wipe and wiped my bottom. Den her used a Clorox wipe to

Clean da floor where I left my deposit, dropped it all in a bag, tied it shut and dropped it in da trash 🗑️. No one was the wiser. I was so relieved 😌 off we went to the next plane. ✈️ We gots to Fort Smith,Arkansas and went to go find Auntie who was picking us up. We gots to Aunties house and you know what ??? Hers has a baby named Gracie. 👶 Gracie was not happy to see me. Her hided in aunties room. She would sneak out and peek 👀 at me. I made it my mission to be her friend, it only took us a few days and we were beat friends. Mommy and daddy had lots to do to da new house. 🏠

We wents to see daddy's cousin up in Bartlesville. It's near Pawhuska. Do yous know who da pioneer woman 👩 is ? Well We wents to her mercantile, den we ate in her restaurant. Oh my goodness mommy said she had never seen a plate that big. Boy oh boy it was delicious 😋 I love Chicken fried steak

I gots to see snow ❄️ for da first time too. I met lots of friends at aunties. Dere was Maggie Moo, Mac a doodle, Boogie bear. 🐾 🐾 🐾 I gots to play wif em
dat was really fun. I is really excited about us living in Okie-homa. Mommy said she is taking all of us back wif her in March. Her said we is going in da go machine 🚗 I thinks she should send

me first class ✈ And I'll meet dem dere. I know Auntie would take care of me until mommy, bossy and Harley gots there. 🐵

Mommy has been busy since we been home in California. My hooman grandpa is really sick. Her has been crying a lot, her says please don't worry about me, her will try to share my adventures more. We are all ok. Bossy, Harley and I have been giving her extra snuggles. I better go, mommy says it's a nice day and we all should spend some time outside enjoying it today.

Paws and kisses,
Monkey Mae

Monkey here !

I wants you alls to know I is scared of da boogie man ! 😴 Hims is really scary 😱 😳 ! I was minding my own Monkey Mae business, being da perfect little angel that I am. 😌 Hey stop laughing! I'm really serious I was being good, dis is not a laughing matter !!!

I was snuggled on da bed wif Harley and Bossy we was sleepin next to MHM and daddy. Daddy was restless cuz hims has woken up early to the sound of Ol man Harley getting sick on da stairs to da bed. Daddy yelled at MHM, hims said quick quick get up Harley is throwing up ! 🤢 MHM sure can move fast 💨 when it is one of us involved. Her flew outa bed 🛏 and grabbed Harley up and gave him a once over before her cleaned him up. Her washed his face and boy was he upset 😾

Him was restless he was turning and tossing and moving da covers all over da bed 🛏 it was super annoying because I needed my Monkey Mae beauty sleeps 😴

Anyhoooo I wasn't the only one who was disturbed, Bossy kept kicking MHM till MHM scootched all da way over to da edge of da bed 🛏

Then it happened! Da Boogie Man 👻 !!! 😱 😳 firsts I heard a rumble. Den I heard a grumble. Den I heard snoring 💤 it sounded like my daddy, I sats up in a bed, I likes to snuggle my daddy where he is nice and warm by his neck early in da morning. Well then I saw it !! 👀 DA BOOGIE MAN !!! 👻 👻 👻 👻 👻 👻 👻 👻

All I saw was 2 eyes 👁 Dey were closed, but yes there were 2 of dem eyes 👁. And I saws a nose 👃 da covers were pulled up right below dat nose 👃. What was that ?!?! It was a boogie man that's what it was !! Bark ! BARK ! BARRRRRRRRRK ! I sounded da Monkey Mae emergency 🚨 alarm 🚨
Bossy started barking, she jumped to her feet. I didn't dare move, dat thing was gonna get me !! Help !!! I'm too cute to die !!! Bark !bark !BARRRRRRKKKK!

MHM said Monkey, Bossy stop it. Den !!! den !!!, da eyes 👁 opened ! Dey were lookin right at me !! MHM started laughing 😂 her was really laughing. Den I heard Daddy laugh 😂 where was daddy ! I needed him. DER WAS A BOOGIE MAN IN DA BED !!! I looked at MHM and barked she laughed harder. She sat up and reached out to the blanket by that boogie mans nose 👃. I couldn't believe my eyes 👀 MHM was going to release the BOOGIE MAN !!! Her was still laughing ! Dis was not amusing ! WOOooosh ! 💨 MHM pulled da blankets down. I couldn't look 👀 🙈

88

MHM and daddy were laughing, where was daddy ? I heard him but..... I peeked at the BOOGIE MAN. I blinked, I blinked again. Focus eyes 👀 FOCUS !! Wait ... what ? Dat was no BOOGIE MAN, dat was daddy ! I jumped for joy ! Daddy !!! I jumped right on his face and started licking 🐻 him all over da face !! Yay Daddy !

Now I am not happy with MHM, her was gonna release da BOOGIE MAN, her is not nice. Now I'm exhausted from my early morning adventure with da Boogie Man. Think 💭 I'll take a nap 🐻

Stay safe friends, protect yourselfs from da Boogie Man 👻

Paws and kisses
🐾 🐾 🐾
Monkey Mae

Hellllooooo everybooty

Yesterday was terrible, MHM dunked us in da suds 🦆 her scrubbed 🧽 🧽 us till we were squeaky clean ! Den her tried to bribe us with cookies 🍪 I helded a grudge, I don't like da suds.

Den MHM her held me down and brushed me ! What da heck did I do to her ??? Whatever it was dat I did I better figure it out so it doesn't happen again.

We gots company too ! Grandpa Larry and Grandma Dixie and their yorkie Millie. Her is a grouchy old lady. Her gets real mad if I get too close to her mommy or daddy. Her shows her teefs 🦷 and looks at me like i is a piece of meat 🍖 !! I is not meat ! I is da Monkey Mae !

Her mommy has to keep her on a leash to control her, I decided I don't wanna be her friend. Her is mean. Her even tried to bite Bossy and poor Harley, hims didn't do nuffin, and her still growled at hims. 😟 so we are being extra careful we walks on out tippy toes around her ! I is countin da days till her goes home to her house 🏠 🚗 🦆 📅

Guess what ?, guess what ? GUESS WHAT !!!!

Today is my Barkday ! I turned 1 !!! MHM got me a cake and it smells Dellllliiiiciouuuussss 😋 Her said her is gonna take pictures 📷 after my cake this evening. I even gots a birthday hat 🎂

🎵 Happy Barkday to me ! Happy Barkday dear Monkey Mae, Happy Barkday to me !!! 🎵

Paws and kisses and Barkday wishes !
🐾 💙 and 🎂

Monkey Mae the fiesty 1 year old .

Bloopers from my first year -

Who doesn't love a lil girl in a tutu ?

Someone get this headband off me !!!

Mhm stealin smooches

Just a girl who loves to nap

What you lookin at Mhm ?

When a bee stung me and Mhm put some ice on it for me

THIS IS WHY I NEED WINGS

THIS CHAIR IS OUT TO GET ME !!!!

Printed in Great Britain
by Amazon